Colour by Heart

Mindful colouring
to relieve stress
Volume 1

Anne Wood

Foreword by
Karen A. Baikie Ph.D

Foreword

I'm pleased to have the opportunity to introduce you to *Colour by Heart: Mindful colouring to relieve stress*. I am a clinical psychologist and mindfulness-based therapist, so I am excited to share with you some thoughts on mindfulness and how this colouring book may assist you in moving towards greater calmness and wellbeing. I loved colouring-in as a child, and I have enjoyed the explosion of adult colouring books, as it gives many of us the opportunity to return to an enjoyable and much-loved activity at the same time as doing something good for ourselves. It's not all that often that we get to do something that is both fun *and* good for us!

What is mindfulness, you may ask? It's become a household word in Western countries in the past decade or so, even though it has been around for a long time. Mindfulness is about paying attention. It is also about being present to whatever is there in the moment – whether that be thoughts, feelings, sensations, impulses, images, memories, or not very much at all. However it is also about being present without judgement – just accepting whatever is there. The idea is to keep coming back to the present, to whatever is there in front of you, even though your mind will no doubt run off to a million other places as you hold the pencil.

So as you colour in, I invite you to notice whatever comes up for you. Perhaps you feel unsure of what colour to use, and you notice yourself deliberating; or you feel like you have to do a good job or finish it completely; or you get frustrated because you keep being distracted by other thoughts that are bothering you, and you get annoyed at yourself because this mindful colouring in is supposed to be relaxing! Maybe you catch yourself remembering times doing craft as a six-year old and smiling. See if you can just be mindful of what you notice, without judging yourself. Be kind and compassionate, rather than harsh or critical with yourself. You can use what happens when you colour in to notice something interesting about yourself. Be curious, and then let it go. Come back to colouring in, and see what comes next. Just keep coming back to the present – to the page, the mandala, your pencils, the colours, and your own breath. That's mindfulness. Moment by moment, keep coming back. It's a practice. Every time you come back to the moment, you are being mindful.

There is a strong connection between the mind and the heart. In fact, in some languages, the word for mind and heart is the same. So perhaps we could say that mindfulness is in fact heartfulness. Practicing mindfulness is a wonderful way to open your heart and develop more compassion in your life. As you colour in the mandalas in Colour by Heart, perhaps you could let the heart in the centre of each mandala remind you to stay mindful and open your heart to whatever shows up for you, and to stay kind and compassionate towards yourself.

I hope that you enjoy colouring the mandalas in Colour by Heart. As we say in my line of work, "There is nothing as useful as mindfulness". Enjoy both your colouring and your personal discoveries along the way.

Warmly,

Dr Karen Baikie
Consultant Clinical Psychologist
Certified Hakomi Therapist and Teacher
Sydney, Australia

Suggestions for use

Children love to draw freehand and colour-in pre-drawn pictures. Indulge the child within you and enjoy colouring the following pages. You can use pencils, pastels, markers or a mixture of these to create the effects you prefer. Shading and contrasting colours make interesting pictures and you can always photocopy the page to colour before you decide on the finished effect. Allow your imagination to run wild and be creative!

The mandalas are deliberately printed on one side only. You can place a clean sheet of paper behind the page you are colouring to further ensure no colour bleeds through the page – depending on what you are using as a colouring medium.

If you want to know more about this craze which is sweeping the world, visit and 'like' the MPowering Publishing Facebook page for updates on all our books.

There will be news there of further books to colour. The next books in the series will include more complicated mandalas for you to colour.

Feel free to give us a review on Amazon if you enjoyed this book.

At the end of the way is

freedom.

Till then, patience.

Buddha

Your mind will be like its

habitual thoughts:

for the soul becomes dyed

with the colour of its thoughts.

Marcus Aurelius

Mistakes are part of the dues

one pays for a full life.

Sophia Loren

Rest with gentle patience and

strength.

Chogyam Trungpa

If you want to be loved,

be lovable.

Ovid

Happiness never decreases

by being shared.

Amitabha Buddhist Society

Creativity is the greatest

rebellion in existence.

Osho

Life is a great big canvas;

throw all the paint on it you can.

Danny Kaye

The factor that sustains

a genuine friendship is

a feeling of affection.

The Dalai Lama

No matter how long the winter,

spring is sure to follow.

Guinean Proverb

Since everything

is a reflection of our minds,

everything can be changed

by our minds.

Amitabha Buddhist Society

Within all beings

there is the seed of perfection.

The Dalai Lama

A lifetime is just long enough to

do something worth doing.

If you get going now.

Charlotte Gray

The way I see it,

if you want the rainbow,

you gotta put up with the rain.

Dolly Parton

Look inside and find where a

person loves from. That's the

reality, not what they say.

Hypocrites

To keep a lamp burning

we have to keep putting oil in it.

Mother Teresa

The secret of all learning

is patience.

Iris Murdoch

The more you praise and

celebrate your life,

the more there is in life

to celebrate.

Oprah Winfrey

The sense of contentment

is a key factor for

attaining happiness.

The Dalai Lama

He is able

who thinks he is able.

Amitabha Buddhist Society

Dear God

These circumstances will change.

This situation will pass.

Amen.

Leunig

In three words I can sum up

everything I have learned

about life:

It goes on.

Robert Frost

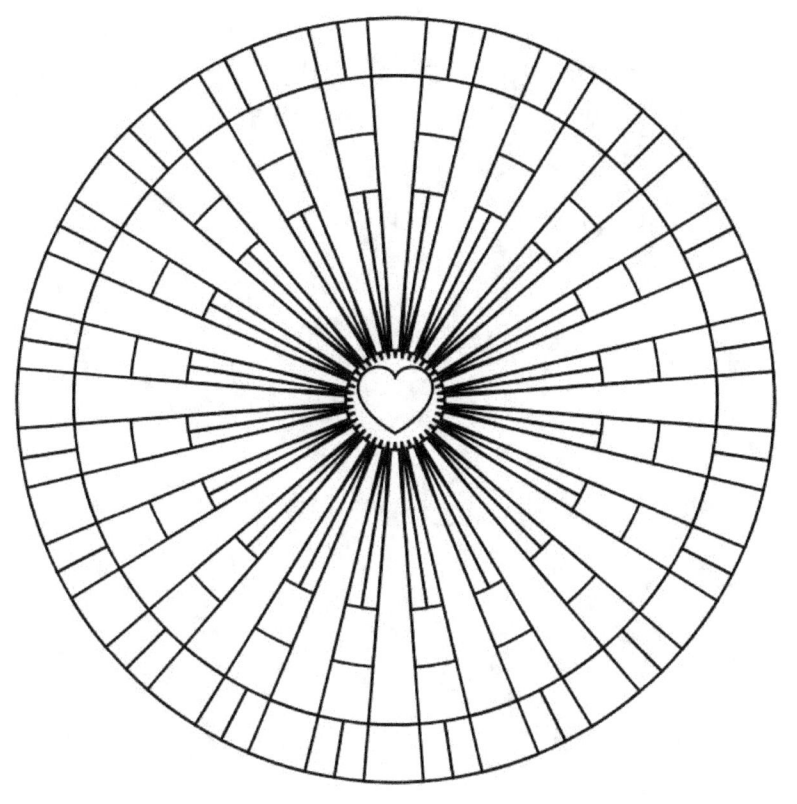

Grey skies are just the

clouds passing over.

Duke Ellington

Worry is interest paid on

trouble before it is due.

Miriam Makeba

Change takes time.

The Dalai Lama

It is our own thoughts that

lead us into trouble,

not other people.

Amitabha Buddhist Society

Go within every day

and find the inner strength

so that the world will not

blow your candle out.

Katherine Dunham

Nothing is so strong as

gentleness and nothing so gentle

as real strength.

St Francis de Sales

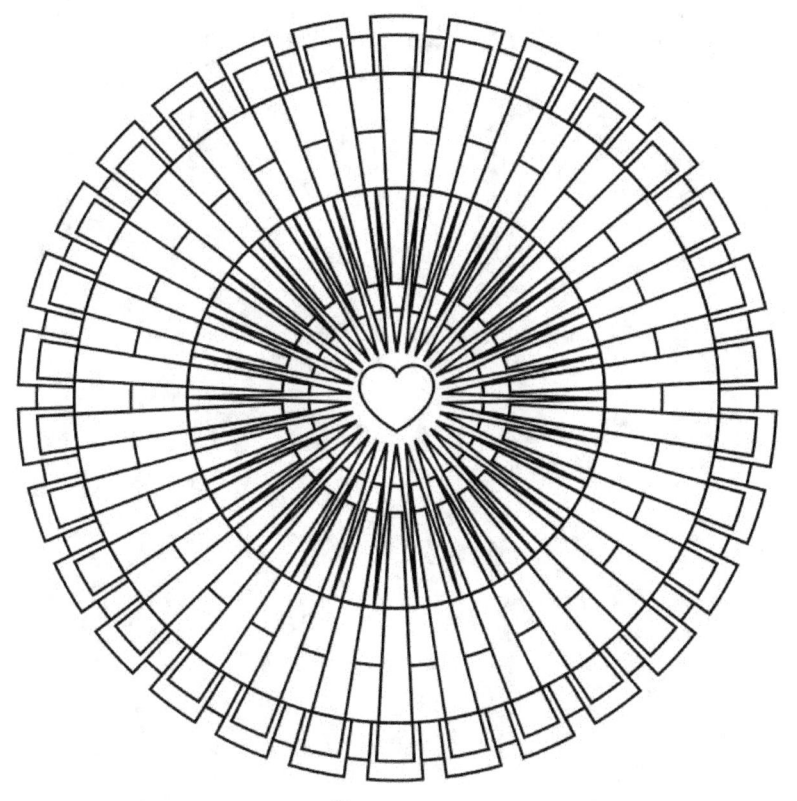

The ability to look at events

from different perspectives

can be very helpful.

The Dalai Lama

Love is never having to say

you're sorry.

Eric Segal.

This page has intentionally been left blank for you to remove and place behind the pages you are colouring to avoid colour bleed.

This page has intentionally been left blank for you to remove and place behind the pages you are colouring to avoid colour bleed.

Have you have enjoyed colouring these designs created for you?

If so, we would love you to leave a review of this book on Amazon so others may be encouraged to enjoy colouring the designs too.

Look out there for more colouring books from Anne Wood to enjoy.